AF715544

# Panama 201: Advanced Strategies for Expats

**The Expat's Path to Panama: From Surviving to Thriving and Beyond, Volume 3**

Elwood Fletcher

Published by Elwood Fletcher, 2025

While every precaution has been taken in the preparation of this book, the publisher assumes no responsibility for errors or omissions, or for damages resulting from the use of the information contained herein.

PANAMA 201: ADVANCED STRATEGIES FOR EXPATS

**First edition. August 4, 2025**

Copyright © 2025 Elwood Fletcher

Written by Elwood Fletcher

# Disclaimer

The information contained in this book is for general informational and educational purposes only. It is not intended as legal, financial, tax, or immigration advice, nor should it be relied upon as such.

**Legal and Immigration Matters:** Panama's visa requirements, immigration laws, and regulations change frequently and can be complex. This guide reflects information available at the time of writing and may not reflect current requirements. Always consult with qualified Panamanian immigration attorneys and official government sources before making any visa or residency decisions.

**Financial Information:** Any financial information, cost estimates, or investment advice provided herein is for informational purposes only and should not be considered personalized financial advice. Consult with qualified financial advisors familiar with both your home country and Panama tax obligations before making financial decisions.

**Individual Results May Vary:** The author's experiences and those shared by others may not reflect your experience. Success in obtaining visas, finding housing, accessing healthcare, or adapting to life in Panama depends on numerous individual factors.

**No Guarantees:** The author makes no representations or warranties about the accuracy, completeness, or suitability of the information contained in this book. The author assumes no responsibility for errors, omissions, or contrary interpretations of the information provided.

**Limitation of Liability:** Under no circumstances shall the author be liable for any direct, indirect, incidental, or consequential damages arising from the use of this information, even if advised of the possibility of such damages.

**Official Sources:** Readers are strongly encouraged to verify all information with official Panamanian government agencies, qualified legal professionals, and other authoritative sources before making any decisions based on the content of this book.
By reading this book, you acknowledge that you understand and accept these limitations and agree to use the information at your own risk.

# Table of Contents

# About the Author

Elwood Fletcher is a retired expat, avid traveler, and self-proclaimed food critic who now calls Panama home. After decades of living a fast-paced life, Elwood traded in the grind for palm trees, tropical breezes, and the vibrant culture of Central America. With his signature Panama hat, Hawaiian shirt, a goatee, and a tropical drink in hand, Elwood is passionate about sharing his experiences with others.

Through his blog, Elwood offers a blend of practical advice, travel stories, and insider tips for those looking to explore Panama, whether for a short stay or a permanent move. His humorous yet down-to-earth writing style brings a fresh perspective on what it's really like to live in Panama, and he's always ready with a friendly word or a piece of wisdom from his very own expat journey.

When Elwood isn't exploring the backroads of Panama or dining at local eateries, he's likely sharing his discoveries with readers, guiding fellow travelers, and enjoying the simple pleasures of expat life.

Join Elwood on his adventure, and learn how to make the most of life in Panama, one tropical drink at a time.

# Introduction

# Strategic Planning for Your Panama Visa: Setting Up Your Investment AND Your Life

Three months after getting my Pensionado Visa approved, I was sitting in a cramped apartment in Panama City, trying to figure out why my internet kept cutting out, wondering if I'd made a terrible mistake with my housing choice, and realizing that I'd spent so much energy on getting the visa that I'd barely thought about what came next.

Don't be me. Don't treat your visa application like a sprint to the finish line, only to discover you've won the right to scramble around a foreign country trying to set up basic life infrastructure from scratch. After watching dozens of expats make this same mistake, I've learned that the smart approach is to use your visa application process as the foundation for building your actual life in Panama.

Whether you're going for the Pensionado, Friendly Nations, or one of the investment visas, you're going to need to put money into Panama anyway. The key is making those required investments work double duty: satisfying visa requirements while setting up the life you want to live. Let me show you how to think strategically about this entire process.

# The Two-Birds-One-Stone Approach

Every Panama visa, except the basic Pensionado, requires you to demonstrate economic ties to the country. Instead of seeing this as a bureaucratic hurdle, think of it as forced financial planning that happens to come with residency benefits.

Take the Friendly Nations Visa, which requires either a $200,000 real estate investment or a $5,000 bank deposit plus a business. Most people focus on meeting the minimum requirements, but the smart play is asking: "What do I need to live comfortably in Panama, and how can I structure that to satisfy the visa requirements?"

Suppose you're planning to live in Panama City and work remotely; that $200,000 real estate investment could be a well-located condo that gives you both visa qualification and eliminates rent payments. If you're thinking about starting a consulting business, that $5,000 deposit becomes your business operating fund while checking the visa box.

The same logic applies to investment visas. The $300,000 requirement for the Self-Economic Solvency Visa can be fulfilled by splitting the amount between a primary residence and a rental property that generates income. You're not just buying a visa; you're building a financial foundation for your new life.

# Real Estate: Location, Location, Visa Application

Real estate is the most popular visa investment for good reason: it's tangible, potentially appreciating, and serves an obvious life purpose. But choosing the right property requires thinking beyond just meeting visa requirements.

**For the Pensionado Visa Holder:**
Although you don't need to buy property for the Pensionado, many people still do. Plan this purchase during your visa application process. You'll already be spending months getting to know Panama, meeting with lawyers, and establishing local connections. Use this time to seriously house hunt instead of rushing into a purchase decision later.

I know a couple from Michigan who spent their six-month Pensionado application period looking at properties in Boquete, David, and Panama City. By the time their visa was approved, they'd already closed on a house in Boquete and had their utilities transferred. They moved from temporary rental to permanent home without missing a beat.

**For Investment Visa Applicants:**
Your property choice becomes even more critical because it's tied to your visa status. Think about your actual living needs first, then find properties that meet both requirements.

If you're planning to spend six months in Panama and six months elsewhere, a condo in an established building with good management makes sense. You want something that won't fall apart while you're gone and doesn't require constant maintenance.

If you're planning to live in Panama full-time, consider properties that could generate rental income. A duplex where you live in one unit and rent the other can help offset living costs while satisfying investment requirements.

**Location Strategy:**
Your property location should align with your banking, healthcare, and social needs. Buying a beach house in Bocas del Toro might sound romantic, but if you need regular medical care, you'll be flying to Panama City constantly. That beautiful mountain retreat in Boquete is perfect until you realize the nearest major bank branch is an hour away.

I recommend the "triangle approach": choose a location that puts you within reasonable distance of quality healthcare, banking services, and either an airport or major city. Panama City satisfies all three. Boquete works if you're okay with driving to David for banking and flying from there for international travel. Bocas del Toro is more challenging unless you're truly embracing the remote lifestyle.

## Banking: Your Financial Command Center

Opening a Panamanian bank account is essential for any visa category, but the timing and approach matter more than most people realize. Don't wait until after your visa is approved; start this process during your application period.

**For Investment Visa Applicants:**
Your required bank deposits need to go into Panamanian banks anyway, so this becomes your entry point into the local banking system. But think beyond just parking money for visa purposes. You'll need checking accounts, online banking, and potentially credit cards for daily life.

Global Bank and Banco General are the most expat-friendly options, with English-speaking staff and online banking systems that work. BAC Credomatic is another good option, especially if you're planning to travel throughout Central America.

**Banking Strategy:**
Open accounts in the city where you plan to live, but also consider having a backup account in Panama City. Even if you're living in Boquete, having a Panama City account makes certain transactions easier and gives you options if you need to handle complex financial matters.

Set up online banking immediately and learn how to use it. Panama's banking system is more cash-dependent than what you're used to, but online banking works well for bill payments and transfers. You'll also want to understand how to wire money internationally, both inbound and outbound.

**Credit Building:**
Start building a Panamanian credit history early. Use your bank's credit card for daily purchases and pay it off monthly. This becomes important later if you want to finance additional property purchases or business investments.

## Healthcare: Beyond the Visa Requirements

Most visa applications require basic health screenings, but thoughtful planning means setting up your complete healthcare system during the application process.

**Choosing Your Healthcare Base:**
Panama has excellent private healthcare, but it's concentrated in certain areas. Panama City has the most comprehensive options, including Hospital Punta Pacifica (Johns Hopkins affiliate) and Hospital San Fernando. David has solid regional healthcare. Smaller cities have basic services but refer complex cases to larger centers.

Your visa investment location should align with your healthcare needs. If you have chronic conditions requiring specialist care, investing in property near major medical centers makes sense. If you're generally healthy and need routine care, you have more flexibility in choosing a location.

**Insurance Strategy:**
Start researching health insurance options during your visa application. You can't purchase local insurance until you have residency, but you can research providers and understand your options.

Private insurance in Panama is excellent and affordable compared to U.S. standards. Companies like Aseguradora Ancón and Mapfre offer comprehensive coverage that includes international emergency evacuation. Many expats supplement this with travel insurance that covers trips back to their home countries.

**Building Medical Relationships:**
Once you have residency, establish relationships with local doctors before you need them. Get routine checkups, establish baseline health records, and make sure your prescription medications are available locally or can be imported easily.

## Business Setup: Making Your Investment Work

If you're using the Friendly Nations Visa business route or starting a company for other visa categories, consider thinking beyond just meeting the minimum requirements. Set up a business that could generate income or provide tax benefits.

**Consulting and Remote Work:**
Many expats set up consulting companies that allow them to work with international clients while maintaining Panamanian residency. This structure can provide tax advantages and satisfy visa requirements.

The key is to ensure that your business activities don't compete with local professionals. Software development, online marketing, and financial consulting for international clients all work well. Local services like accounting or legal work would require additional licensing and permits.

**Rental Property Management:**
If you're buying multiple properties for investment visa purposes, consider setting up a property management company. This formalizes your real estate investments as a business and could

generate additional income if you manage properties for other expats.

**Import/Export Opportunities:**
Panama's position as a logistics hub creates opportunities for small-scale import/export businesses. This could be as simple as importing specialty products from your home country for the local expat market.

## Infrastructure: The Boring but Essential Stuff

While you're focused on major decisions, such as property and banking, don't forget the mundane infrastructure that makes daily life possible.

**Utilities and Services:**
Set up utilities in your name as soon as you have a permanent address. This includes electricity, water, internet, and phone service. Having these in your name helps establish your residency history and makes future applications easier.

Internet service varies dramatically by location. Cable Onda, Tigo, and +Movil are the leading providers, but service quality depends heavily on your specific area. Research this before choosing where to live, especially if you're planning to work remotely.

**Transportation:**
Getting your Panamanian driver's license should be a priority once you have residency. This process takes time and requires specific documentation; therefore, it is advisable to start early. Your license becomes an essential piece of identification for banking, healthcare, and other services.

If you're planning to buy a vehicle, research the local market during your visa application period. Understanding import duties, registration requirements, and insurance options helps you budget accurately.

**Legal and Professional Services:**
Build relationships with local professionals during your visa application process. You'll need ongoing relationships with lawyers, accountants, and potentially property managers. The lawyers handling your visa application can often provide referrals for other services.

## Tax Planning: The Often-Overlooked Piece

Panama's tax system offers advantages for residents, but maximizing these benefits requires planning during your visa application process, not after.

**Territorial Tax System:**
Panama only taxes income earned within Panama. For many expats, this means significant tax savings on foreign-sourced income like pensions, investment returns, or remote work income. But structuring this correctly requires advanced planning.

**Business Structure Optimization:**
If you're setting up a business for visa purposes, consider how this affects your tax situation. Panamanian corporations can provide tax advantages for certain types of income, but the structure needs to be set up correctly from the beginning.

**U.S. Tax Considerations:**
American expats still need to file U.S. tax returns and may need to report foreign bank accounts and businesses. Plan for this complexity by establishing relationships with tax professionals who understand both systems.

# Timeline Integration: Coordinating Everything

The key to strategic planning is coordinating all these elements with your visa application timeline. Here's how to think about sequencing:

**Months 1-2: Foundation Building**

- Choose your investment location and property type
- Begin banking relationships and account setup
- Research healthcare options and insurance
- Start building a local professional network

**Months 3-4: Major Decisions**

- Finalize property purchases or business setup
- Complete banking requirements for a visa
- Establish healthcare relationships
- Begin utility and service setup

**Months 5-6: Integration**

- Complete visa application with all investments in place
- Finalize insurance and healthcare arrangements
- Establish routine services and infrastructure
- Plan for post-approval integration

**Post-Approval: Optimization**

- Optimize tax strategies with established residency
- Expand business activities if desired
- Build long-term financial relationships
- Establish routine maintenance for all systems

## Common Mistakes to Avoid

**The Minimum Compliance Trap:**
Don't just meet visa requirements; build a foundation for the life you want. That $200,000 investment should serve your actual needs, not just check a bureaucratic box.

**The Location Mismatch:**
Don't buy property in one location just because it's cheap if you plan to live elsewhere. Your visa investment should align with your lifestyle preferences.

**The Infrastructure Afterthought:**
Don't treat banking, healthcare, and utilities as post-approval problems. These take time to set up correctly and affect your quality of life from day one.

**The Tax Procrastination:**
Don't ignore tax planning until after you have residency. The opportunities for optimization are better when planned from the beginning.

## Your Strategic Checklist

Before you start your visa application, ask yourself:

- Where do I want to live in Panama?
- What are my ongoing healthcare needs?
- How do I want to structure my finances?
- What business activities interest me?
- How will this affect my tax situation?

Use your visa application period to answer these questions through action, not just research. Visit different locations, meet with professionals, and start building the infrastructure you'll need.

The goal isn't just to get a visa; it's to build a life in Panama that's better than what you're leaving behind. With strategic planning, your visa investments become the foundation for that better life, not just the price of admission.

By the time your visa is approved, you should be ready to step into a life you've already started building, not scrambling to figure out necessities in a foreign country. That's the difference between getting a visa and getting a life.

# Chapter 1

# Year Two Financial Optimization: Advanced Tax Strategies, Investment Opportunities, and Currency Management

I was sitting in my accountant's office in Panama City, staring at a stack of documents that would make a tax attorney weep, when I realized something important: surviving your first year in Panama is one thing, but optimizing your financial life here is an entirely different game. The honeymoon phase of "wow, everything is so cheap" had worn off, and I was face-to-face with the reality that savvy expats don't just live in Panama, they build wealth here.

If you've made it through your first year, congratulations. You've figured out where to buy groceries without getting lost, you know which potholes to avoid on your daily routes, and you've probably learned enough Spanish to argue with the cable company. But now comes the real challenge: making your money work as hard for you as you worked to get here in the first place.

Welcome to Panama 201, where we explore the financial strategies that distinguish tourists from residents, and residents from those who are truly building something lasting in this country.

## The Second-Year Reality Check

Your first year in Panama was about survival and adjustment. You spent money on setup costs, overpaid for things because you didn't know better, and probably made a few financial decisions that seemed smart at the time but now make you wince. That's normal, and if you're being honest with yourself about those mistakes, you're already ahead of most expats who never get past the "everything's cheap" mentality.

But here's what changes in year two: you start to understand not just what things cost, but what they're worth. You learn the difference between expensive and overpriced. You begin to notice opportunities that weren't apparent when you were struggling to pay your electric bill without waiting in line for three hours.

The financial landscape in Panama offers genuine advantages for people who know how to use them, but these advantages aren't automatic. They require planning, patience, and a willingness to think differently about money than you did back home. The expats who thrive financially here are those who have stopped thinking like visitors and started thinking like investors.

## Understanding Panama's Tax Environment

Panama operates on a territorial tax system, which sounds simple until you attempt to navigate it. The basic principle is straightforward: Panama only taxes income generated within Panama's borders. Income from outside sources, your U.S. pension, rental properties back home, and investment dividends from foreign companies aren't subject to Panamanian income tax.

The devil, as always, is in the details. What counts as "foreign source" income isn't always obvious, and the rules have nuances that can either save you thousands or cost you dearly if you get them wrong. If you're providing services to clients outside Panama but performing the work while sitting in your Panama City apartment, where was that income generated? The answer matters, and it's not always intuitive.

This is where professional help becomes essential, not optional. I learned this lesson the expensive way when I assumed my online consulting work was automatically foreign source income. The reality was more complicated, and sorting it out required both a good local accountant and a tax attorney who understood the intricacies of Panama's system.

The key insight here is that Panama's territorial tax system creates opportunities, but only for people who structure their affairs correctly from the beginning. Trying to retrofit tax efficiency after you've already established patterns and relationships is like trying to renovate a house while living in it; it's possible, but messy and expensive.

## Residency Status and Tax Implications

Your residency status affects more than just your ability to stay in the country legally. It fundamentally changes your tax obligations, both in Panama and potentially in your home country. Most people understand this in theory, but few grasp the practical implications until they're facing their second year of tax filings.

If you're on a pensionado visa, you're considered a Panamanian tax resident, which means you're subject to Panamanian tax law on your worldwide income generated within Panama's borders. However, maintaining your tax obligations in your home country also creates a web of compliance requirements that can be overwhelming to handle on your own.

The United States, for example, requires citizens to file tax returns regardless of where they live or earn their money. This creates situations where you need to understand both systems well enough to avoid double taxation while ensuring compliance with both sets of rules. The foreign earned income exclusion, foreign tax credits, and treaty provisions all come into play, and getting any of these wrong can be costly.

I've seen many expats attempt to use tax software designed for domestic situations, only to create problems that take years and significant expense to resolve. The money you save by avoiding professional help in the first year usually costs you multiples of that savings in later years.

## Investment Opportunities in Panama

Panama's banking system offers investment opportunities that many expats never discover because they're too focused on the challenges of basic banking to explore the possibilities. Once you've established relationships with local banks and understand how the system works, you can access investment products that might surprise you.

Panamanian banks offer term deposits with rates that are often more attractive than those found in the United States, especially in the current interest rate environment. These aren't exotic investments, they're traditional bank products with FDIC-equivalent insurance through Panama's deposit insurance system. The catch is that the best rates are often reserved for established customers with substantial balances and a proven track record of relationships.

The country's real estate market presents opportunities for people who understand local dynamics, but it's not the simple appreciation play that many expats assume. Successful real estate investors here focus on rental yields and understand the specific market segments that consistently generate returns. Tourist rental properties in established areas can provide solid income streams, but they require active management and a deep understanding of both the tourist market and local regulations.

What surprised me most was discovering Panama's position as a regional financial center. The country hosts branches of major international banks, and sophisticated financial products are available for investors who meet the qualification thresholds. Private banking services, offshore investment platforms, and structured products all exist here, but accessing them requires both significant assets and the patience to navigate institutions that operate differently from their U.S. counterparts.

## Currency Dynamics and Practical Management

Living in a dollarized economy eliminates currency exchange risk but creates other considerations that most expats don't anticipate. Panama uses the U.S. dollar as its currency, but the coins are Panamanian, and the practical implications of this hybrid system affect your daily financial life in ways you might not expect.

The lack of currency risk means you don't have to worry about exchange rate fluctuations affecting your purchasing power. Still, it also means you can't benefit from currency depreciation to stretch your dollar further. What you see is what you get, which makes financial planning more straightforward but also means you need to be more thoughtful about where and how you spend your money.

Banking relationships become crucial in ways that aren't immediately apparent. While Panama uses the U.S. dollar, transferring money between U.S. banks and Panamanian banks involves international wire transfers, which come with associated fees, delays, and documentation requirements. Efficient money management requires establishing the right mix of accounts in both countries and understanding when and how to move funds between them.

I've found that maintaining a strategic balance between U.S. and Panamanian banking relationships provides the most flexibility. Some expenses are easier to pay from U.S. accounts, while others benefit from local banking relationships. Online services, U.S. subscriptions, and certain international transactions work more efficiently with U.S. bank accounts, while local utilities, rent, and day-to-day expenses are better handled through Panamanian banks.

# Building Long-Term Wealth Strategies

The most successful expats I know in Panama think beyond just living here; they build wealth here. This requires a fundamental shift in perspective from consumer to investor, from someone who lives in Panama to someone who has integrated their financial life into the country's economic system.

Real estate ownership, whether for personal use or investment, becomes a cornerstone of many successful long-term financial strategies. Property ownership provides stability, potential appreciation, and tax advantages that can be significant over time. However, wise property investment in this region requires an understanding of local market cycles, regulatory environments, and the specific dynamics of different areas and property types.

Business ownership represents another wealth-building opportunity, particularly for expats who can bridge the gap between international markets and local capabilities. Service businesses catering to the growing expat community, import-export operations that leverage Panama's strategic location, and technology companies that can operate globally from Panama's favorable business environment all represent potential wealth-building opportunities.

The key insight is that Panama's economic advantages, territorial taxation, dollarized currency, strategic location, and growing expat community create opportunities for people who approach them strategically rather than accidentally. The expats who build significant wealth here are the ones who saw these advantages coming and positioned themselves to benefit from them.

# Professional Relationships That Matter

None of this happens in a vacuum, and one of the most important investments you'll make in your second year is building relationships with the right professionals. A competent local accountant isn't just helpful, they're essential for navigating tax obligations, understanding reporting requirements, and identifying opportunities you might miss on your own.

Legal counsel becomes essential as you move beyond fundamental residency issues and start making significant financial commitments. Real estate transactions, business formation, and complex tax situations all require legal expertise that's specific to Panama's system. The money you invest in quality professional relationships pays dividends for years through better decisions, avoided problems, and opportunities you might otherwise miss.

Banking relationships require more attention and cultivation than you might expect coming from the United States. Personal relationships with bank officers can make the difference between smooth transactions and bureaucratic nightmares. Taking time to understand your bankers, their processes, and their institutional culture pays practical dividends every time you need to accomplish something complex.

Insurance and financial planning professionals who understand both Panama's system and the complexities of expat financial life are invaluable. They can help you navigate the intersection of two or more countries' financial systems, ensure proper coverage for your specific situation, and identify opportunities for optimization that might not be obvious to someone trying to manage everything themselves.

# Looking Forward

Financial optimization in Panama isn't about getting rich quickly; it's about building a sustainable, efficient financial life that takes advantage of the genuine opportunities this country offers. The expats who succeed financially here are those who approach it systematically, invest in proper professional relationships, and think strategically about their long-term goals rather than just their immediate needs.

Your second year marks the transition from surviving in Panama to thriving here. The financial strategies you implement now will determine whether you're still watching every penny in year five or whether you've built something that provides security and opportunity for the long term.

The next chapter will dive into advanced real estate strategies, including how to evaluate investment properties, understand rental markets, and navigate the legal complexities of property ownership as a foreign investor. Because once you've optimized your tax situation and established proper banking relationships, real estate becomes the next frontier for building wealth in Panama.

But that's a conversation for next time. For now, start thinking about your financial life here not as an extension of what you had back home, but as something entirely new that you're building from scratch. The opportunities are real, but they require intention, planning, and the wisdom to seek help from people who understand both the possibilities and the pitfalls.

The difference between expats who stumble through their financial lives here and those who build something meaningful isn't luck; it's approach. And you're already ahead of the game by thinking about it systematically.

# Chapter 2

# Advanced Real Estate Strategies That Go Beyond Finding a Place to Live

I was standing in a half-finished condo in Costa del Este, listening to a developer explain why this particular unit was going to appreciate 30% within two years, when I realized I was about to make the same mistake that derails most expat real estate investors in Panama. I was thinking like someone who wanted to buy property rather than someone who understood property markets.

The developer was professional, the building looked impressive, and the financing terms seemed reasonable. Everything about the presentation was designed to make the purchase feel inevitable rather than strategic. But after eighteen months in Panama, I had learned enough to ask the questions that most expats never think to ask: who buys units in this building, what do comparable rentals generate for income, and why is this developer so confident about appreciation in this specific market segment?

Those questions led to very different answers than I expected, and ultimately to a very different investment decision. More importantly, they marked the transition from thinking about real estate as a place to live to understanding it as a wealth-building tool in Panama's unique market environment.

If you're ready to move beyond just finding somewhere to call home and start thinking strategically about real estate as an investment, you're about to discover opportunities that most expats never see and pitfalls that can be expensive to learn the hard way.

# Understanding Panama's Real Estate Markets (Plural)

The biggest mistake expats make with Panama real estate is treating it like a single market with consistent rules and dynamics. In reality, Panama has multiple distinct real estate markets that operate according to entirely different principles, serve different customer bases, and offer different risk-reward profiles for investors.

The Panama City high-rise market, which dominates expat real estate conversations, is just one segment, and it's often not the most profitable one for individual investors. These gleaming towers in Punta Pacifica and Costa del Este receive all the attention because they're visible, professionally marketed, and familiar to North Americans accustomed to urban condo living. But they're also highly competitive, developer-driven markets where individual investors compete against sophisticated international buyers and institutional money.

Beach communities like Coronado, Pedasi, and areas along the Pacific coast operate according to entirely different dynamics. Vacation rental demand, seasonal occupancy patterns, and the specific preferences of varying expat demographics drive these markets. A strategy that works in Panama City can be entirely wrong for beach properties, and vice versa.

Then there are the emerging markets in places like Boquete, El Valle, and mountain communities where long-term residents are driving demand for properties that serve as primary residences rather than investments. These markets move more slowly but can offer better value for buyers who understand local preferences and aren't trying to time short-term appreciation cycles.

The key insight is that successful real estate investors in Panama first select their market segment, then find properties within that segment, rather than falling in love with specific properties and hoping the market dynamics work out in their favor.

## Investment Property Economics That Work

Most expat real estate discussions in Panama focus on appreciation potential, which is precisely the opposite of how successful investors approach the market. Appreciation is a bonus, not a strategy. The foundation of profitable real estate investing in this area is rental yield, and calculating realistic rental yields requires an understanding of local market dynamics that aren't immediately apparent to newcomers.

A $200,000 condo in Costa del Este that rents for $1,200 per month might seem like a reasonable 7.2% gross yield until you factor in condo fees, property taxes, management costs, and realistic occupancy rates. Once you account for these factors, your actual return might be closer to 4%, which is barely better than bank CDs and comes with significantly more risk and management hassle.

But a $150,000 house in a well-located neighborhood outside Panama City that rents for $1,000 per month to a long-term tenant might generate a much better risk-adjusted return with less volatility and fewer ongoing headaches. Although the gross yield appears lower, the net yield and long-term stability are potentially significantly better.

The vacation rental market adds another layer of complexity and opportunity. A $180,000 beach condo that rents for $120 per night might generate $2,000 to $3,000 per month during peak season, but might sit empty for months during slower periods. The annual income could be excellent, but the cash flow volatility requires careful financial planning and realistic reserves.

Successful real estate investors here run the numbers based on conservative occupancy assumptions, factor in all costs, including management and maintenance, and focus on properties that generate positive cash flow from day one rather than betting on appreciation to make the investment worthwhile.

## Financing Strategies and Local Banking Relationships

Real estate financing in Panama operates differently from that in the United States, and understanding these differences can mean the difference between profitable investments and costly mistakes. Local banks offer mortgages to foreign residents, but the terms, requirements, and processes are distinctly Panamanian.

Most local banks require down payments of 30-40% for foreign buyers, with interest rates that vary based on your banking relationship, income verification, and the specific property. But here's what most expats don't realize: the bank you choose for your mortgage can be more important than the interest rate they offer, because ongoing banking relationships affect everything from property management to investment opportunities.

Some banks specialize in expat real estate and have streamlined processes for foreign buyers. In contrast, others treat every foreign mortgage application like a special case that requires multiple approvals and extensive documentation. The difference in processing time and hassle can be enormous, and the banks with the best expat processes aren't always the ones with the lowest advertised rates.

Developer financing represents another option that many expats overlook. Established developers often offer financing terms that are more flexible than traditional banks, especially for pre-construction purchases. These arrangements can include lower down payments, extended payment schedules, and terms that are tied to construction milestones rather than traditional mortgage structures.

The key is understanding that financing isn't just about getting money; it's about building relationships with institutions that can support your long-term real estate strategy. The bank that finances your first property might also be the one that helps you expand your portfolio, provides construction loans for renovation projects, or offers investment services for the cash flow your properties generate.

## Legal Structures and Ownership Strategies

Property ownership in Panama involves legal structures that many North Americans are unfamiliar with, and selecting the proper ownership structure can have significant implications for taxes, liability, and future flexibility. The decision between individual ownership, corporate ownership, and various trust structures isn't just legal, it's strategic.

Individual ownership is the most straightforward approach and works well for primary residences or single investment properties. The process is straightforward, the ongoing compliance requirements are minimal, and the tax implications are clear. But individual ownership also means personal liability, limited privacy, and potential complications for estate planning or future property transfers.

Corporate ownership through a Panamanian corporation offers significant advantages for investors who plan to own multiple properties or want to structure their ownership for tax efficiency. Panamanian corporations can own property, provide liability protection, and create opportunities for more sophisticated financial planning. However, corporate ownership also entails annual compliance requirements, increased administrative costs, and ongoing legal and accounting support.

Trust structures represent the most sophisticated option, providing excellent asset protection, estate planning benefits, and tax optimization opportunities. But trusts also require the most professional management and are typically only cost-effective for larger real estate portfolios or investors with complex international financial situations.

The choice between these structures depends on your specific circumstances, long-term plans, and risk tolerance. What's crucial is making this decision before you start buying property, because changing ownership structures after the fact is expensive and complicated. This is one area where investing in quality legal advice upfront can save money and create opportunities for years to come.

## Market Timing and Strategic Positioning

Real estate markets in Panama move in cycles, just like everywhere else, but these cycles are driven by different factors than what most North Americans expect. Understanding these cycles and positioning yourself strategically can mean the difference between buying at peaks and taking advantage of opportunities.

Panama City's high-rise market is heavily influenced by international investment flows, economic conditions in Venezuela and Colombia, as well as government infrastructure projects. Significant developments, such as metro expansion, airport improvements, or new highway construction, can have a substantial impact on property values, but these effects aren't always immediate or obvious.

Beach markets are more closely tied to tourism patterns, seasonal demand cycles, and the specific preferences of different expat demographics. The factors that drive demand in Coronado are different from those that affect Pedasi, and timing your purchases based on local market conditions rather than general economic trends can provide significant advantages.

Mountain communities like Boquete have their dynamics, often tied to North American retirement patterns, seasonal residence preferences, and infrastructure development that affects accessibility and livability. These markets can be less volatile than urban or beach markets, but they also move more slowly and require different investment strategies.

The key insight is that market timing in Panama requires an understanding of local factors rather than applying general real estate investment principles. The investors who do best here are those who pay attention to local market indicators, build relationships with individuals who understand regional dynamics, and position themselves to take advantage of opportunities as they arise, rather than trying to time markets based on external economic indicators.

## Due Diligence That Prevents Expensive Mistakes

Property due diligence in Panama requires attention to details that may not be obvious to buyers from other countries, and skipping steps in the due diligence process can lead to expensive problems that are difficult to resolve after closing. The successful investors I know here are obsessive about due diligence because they understand that preventing problems is much cheaper than fixing them later.

Title verification involves more than just confirming ownership. You need to verify that all property taxes are up to date, that there are no outstanding liens or encumbrances, and that any previous transfers were correctly completed. The property registry system in Panama is generally reliable; however, complex ownership histories or properties that have changed hands multiple times can have hidden issues that aren't immediately apparent.

Physical inspections must account for tropical climate conditions, construction standards that may differ from what you're accustomed to, and infrastructure issues that can impact long-term property performance. Electrical systems, plumbing, roofing, and structural elements all need to be evaluated based on local conditions and standards rather than expectations from temperate climates.

Neighborhood analysis requires understanding factors that affect both livability and investment performance. Traffic patterns, utility reliability, security considerations, and future development plans all impact property values and rental potential. A neighborhood that seems perfect during your weekend visit might have issues that are only apparent to people who live there full-time.

Financial verification means confirming all costs associated with ownership, including property taxes, condo fees, utility costs, and any special assessments or ongoing maintenance obligations. Properties that seem attractively priced sometimes carry hidden costs that significantly impact the total cost of ownership.

## Building a Real Estate Portfolio Strategy

Individual property purchases are tactics. Portfolio strategy is what determines long-term wealth-building success in Panama's real estate market. The expats who build significant real estate wealth here think beyond individual deals and focus on creating portfolios that provide diversification, cash flow, and long-term appreciation potential.

Geographic diversification within Panama can protect against local market downturns while taking advantage of different growth cycles. A portfolio that includes properties in Panama City, a beach location, and a mountain community provides exposure to various market segments and other types of demand drivers.

Property type diversification means balancing different risk-reward profiles within your portfolio. Long-term rental properties provide steady cash flow, while vacation rentals can generate higher yields with more management requirements. Development projects, on the other hand, can offer significant appreciation potential but come with higher risk profiles.

Cash flow management becomes crucial as your portfolio grows. Properties that generate positive cash flow can fund the acquisition of properties that may be cash flow neutral but offer better appreciation potential. The key is to ensure that your overall portfolio generates sufficient positive cash flow to support expansion while building equity for future opportunities.

Professional management becomes increasingly important as your portfolio grows beyond what you can manage personally. Building relationships with property managers, maintenance contractors, and other service providers early in your investment journey creates the infrastructure needed to support portfolio growth without requiring your constant personal attention.

## Working with Local Professionals

Real estate success in Panama requires building relationships with local professionals who understand both the market dynamics and the legal requirements that affect foreign investors. The money you invest in quality professional relationships pays dividends through better opportunities, avoided problems, and more efficient transactions.

Real estate attorneys in Panama do more than handle closings; they can provide market insights, help structure transactions for tax efficiency, and identify potential problems before they become expensive mistakes. The best real estate attorneys here specialize in foreign investor transactions and are well-versed in both Panamanian law and the concerns of international buyers.

Qualified real estate agents can provide access to properties and market intelligence that aren't available through public listings. However, the keyword is 'qualified.' The agent who sold you your first home might not be the right person to help you build an investment portfolio. Look for agents who specialize in investment properties and have experience working with serious investors rather than just assisting expats to find places to live.

Property managers become essential as your portfolio grows, but finding good property managers requires understanding what distinguishes professional property management from casual rental assistance. The best property managers here treat real estate investment as a business, providing detailed financial reporting, proactive maintenance, and professional tenant relations.

Accountants who understand real estate investment taxation can help optimize your investment structure, ensure proper reporting compliance, and identify opportunities for tax efficiency that can significantly impact your overall returns. Real estate taxation in Panama involves nuances that can be easily overlooked without professional guidance.

## Long-Term Wealth Building Through Real Estate

The most successful real estate investors in Panama think beyond individual property appreciation and focus on building wealth through cash flow, tax advantages, and strategic portfolio development. This requires a fundamental shift from thinking of real estate as merely buying property to thinking of it as building a business.

A cash flow focus means prioritizing properties that generate positive monthly income from the start, rather than relying on appreciation to make investments profitable. Properties that pay for themselves while building equity provide the foundation for portfolio expansion and long-term wealth building.

Tax optimization involves structuring your real estate investments to take advantage of Panama's territorial tax system while managing any obligations in your home country. This might include timing property sales to optimize tax treatment, using depreciation to offset other income, or structuring ownership to minimize tax obligations.

Leverage management involves utilizing financing strategically to optimize returns while maintaining sustainable debt levels. The goal isn't to minimize debt, it's to use debt efficiently to accelerate wealth building while maintaining financial stability.

Exit planning involves thinking about how you'll eventually monetize your real estate investments, whether through sales, refinancing, or passing properties to heirs. The best investors here make decisions today that create maximum flexibility for future exit strategies.

## Looking Forward

Real estate in Panama offers genuine opportunities for wealth building. Still, success requires understanding local market dynamics, building professional relationships, and thinking strategically about portfolio development rather than just individual property purchases. The expats who build significant real estate wealth here are those who approached it as a business rather than a hobby.

Your real estate strategy should align with your overall financial goals and capitalize on Panama's specific opportunities while mitigating its unique risks. This means understanding local markets, working with qualified professionals, and focusing on fundamentals such as cash flow and portfolio diversification, rather than chasing short-term appreciation or following expat folklore about guaranteed returns.

The next chapter will explore business opportunities and entrepreneurship strategies for expats who want to generate income in Panama rather than just managing money earned elsewhere. Because once you've optimized your tax situation and built a real estate portfolio, creating local income streams becomes the next frontier for building long-term wealth and security.

But that's a conversation for next time. For now, start thinking about real estate not as a place to live or a single investment decision, but as a strategic component of your overall wealth-building plan in Panama. The opportunities are real, but they require intention, professional support, and a long-term perspective that goes beyond just finding a good deal on a nice property.

# Chapter 3

# Business Opportunities and Income Generation, Building Revenue Streams in Panama

I was having lunch with another expat at a restaurant in Casco Viejo when he casually mentioned that his "little side business" helping other expats navigate government paperwork was generating more income than his U.S. pension. What started as informal help for friends had evolved into a legitimate consulting business that leveraged his hard-earned expertise with Panama's bureaucratic systems.

That conversation was my introduction to a reality that many second-year expats discover: Panama offers genuine opportunities to generate income, but these opportunities often bear little resemblance to traditional employment back home. The expats who build successful income streams here are those who identify problems that need solving, leverage their unique skills and knowledge, and structure their businesses to take advantage of Panama's economic environment.

The key insight isn't that Panama is a gold mine of business opportunities; it's that the country's growing expat community, strategic location, and business-friendly policies create specific niches where informed entrepreneurs can build sustainable income streams. However, success requires understanding local market dynamics, regulatory requirements, and the particular advantages that come with operating a business in Panama.

If you're ready to move beyond managing money earned elsewhere and start generating income in your new home country, you're about to discover opportunities that most expats never see and strategies that can transform your financial security in Panama.

## Understanding Panama's Business Environment

Panama's economy operates on fundamentals that create opportunities for expat entrepreneurs who understand how to position themselves strategically. The country serves as a bridge between North and South America, hosts a growing service sector, and maintains business policies designed to attract international investment and expertise.

The service economy dominates Panama's business landscape, creating opportunities for expats who can provide professional services, consulting, or specialized knowledge that isn't readily available locally. Unlike manufacturing or agriculture, service businesses can often be started with minimal capital investment and can scale based on expertise rather than physical infrastructure.

Panama's territorial tax system provides significant advantages for businesses that generate income from international sources. If you can structure your business to serve clients outside Panama while operating from Panama, you may be able to avoid Panamanian income tax on much of your revenue. This tax advantage can make the difference between a marginally profitable business and a highly successful one.

The growing expat community creates both customers and competition for expat-owned businesses. Understanding this market dynamic is crucial because businesses that serve only other expats have limited growth potential. In contrast, businesses that can serve both expats and locals, or that can utilize Panama as a base for regional operations, have much greater scalability. Regulatory complexity varies significantly by business type, and understanding these differences early in your planning process can save you months of delays and thousands of dollars in compliance costs. Some businesses can be started with minimal bureaucracy, while others require extensive permits, professional certifications, or ongoing regulatory compliance that might not be obvious until you're deep into the process.

## High-Potential Service Business Opportunities

The most successful expat businesses in Panama tend to be service-based operations that leverage expertise, language skills, or cultural knowledge that's valuable but not readily available in the local market. These businesses often begin as informal consulting services but can evolve into substantial operations.

Immigration and relocation consulting represents a significant opportunity for expats who have successfully navigated Panama's systems and can help others avoid the mistakes and delays that often plague newcomers. This business requires extensive knowledge of current procedures, strong relationships with key professionals, and the ability to guide clients through complex processes that are subject to frequent changes.

Real estate services, including property management, rental management, and investment consulting, benefit from the growing expat population and Panama's active real estate market. Success in this sector requires understanding both the technical aspects of property management and the specific needs of expat property owners who may be managing assets from a distance.

Business formation and ongoing compliance services cater to the increasing number of expatriates who wish to establish businesses in Panama but lack understanding of the regulatory requirements and ongoing obligations. This opportunity requires developing expertise in Panama's business laws and building relationships with accountants, attorneys, and government offices that can support client needs.

Translation and interpretation services remain in high demand, particularly for specialized business or legal contexts where accuracy is crucial. This business can start as freelance work but can evolve into an agency model that serves corporate clients, law firms, or government contractors who require reliable language services.

Financial services, including tax preparation, bookkeeping, and financial planning, serve expats who need assistance managing their finances across multiple countries. This business requires proper certification and insurance, as the demand is substantial because most local accountants don't understand the complexities of expat financial situations.

## International Business Models from Panama

Panama's strategic location and business-friendly policies make it an excellent base for businesses that serve international markets rather than just local ones. These models often offer better growth potential and can capitalize on Panama's territorial tax benefits.

Digital marketing and online business services can be operated from Panama while serving clients worldwide. The time zone alignment with North American business hours, reliable internet infrastructure, and lower operating costs create competitive advantages for businesses that provide web development, digital marketing, content creation, or online business services.

Import-export operations leverage Panama's position as a regional trade hub and the expertise that many expats bring from their home countries. Successful operations often focus on specific product categories or market segments where the operator has specialized knowledge or established relationships.

Consulting services that draw on professional expertise from your previous career can often be delivered internationally from

Panama. Whether it's engineering consulting, business strategy, technology implementation, or industry-specific knowledge, many consulting services can be provided remotely while leveraging Panama's lower operating costs.

Online education and training businesses benefit from Panama's growing reputation as an expat destination and the demand for expertise about living and doing business in Latin America. These businesses can serve both aspiring expats and existing residents who want to develop specific skills.

Regional representation services for North American or European companies seeking to expand into Latin American markets offer opportunities for expatriates with relevant industry experience and language skills. These arrangements can range from informal consulting to formal distributor relationships.

## Tourism and Hospitality Ventures

Panama's growing tourism industry creates opportunities for expat entrepreneurs who understand both international visitor expectations and local market dynamics. These businesses often require more capital investment but can provide substantial returns in the right locations.

Vacation rental management services cater to the growing number of property owners who wish to rent out their properties but prefer not to handle the day-to-day management responsibilities. This business model benefits from Panama's year-round tourism season and the increasing popularity of vacation rentals over traditional hotels.

Specialized tour services that cater to specific interests or demographics can be highly profitable because they command premium pricing while serving underserved market segments. Examples include bird-watching tours, fishing charters, cultural immersion experiences, or adventure tourism tailored to specific age groups or skill levels.

Restaurant and hospitality businesses can succeed by serving underserved markets or providing exceptional quality in competitive markets. Many successful expat-owned restaurants focus on cuisine that isn't readily available locally or provide dining experiences that cater to international visitors and expat residents.

Event planning and destination wedding services take advantage of Panama's growing reputation as a wedding and event destination. These businesses require strong organizational skills and local vendor relationships but can generate substantial revenue from high-value events.

Transportation services, including airport transfers, tour transportation, and specialized logistics, cater to both tourists and residents who require reliable and professional transportation. Success in this sector requires proper licensing, insurance, and vehicles that are suitable for local conditions.

## Technology and Online Opportunities

Panama's improving internet infrastructure and favorable business environment make it an attractive location for technology-based businesses that can serve both local and international markets. These opportunities often require specialized skills but can offer excellent scalability.

Software development and technology consulting can take advantage of Panama's lower operating costs while serving international clients who value English-language communication and North American business practices. The time zone alignment with U.S. markets provides significant advantages for businesses that need real-time collaboration.

E-commerce operations that import products for sale throughout Latin America can leverage Panama's trade infrastructure and strategic location. Success requires understanding regional market preferences, logistics systems, and regulatory requirements for different product categories.

Digital content creation, including blogging, YouTube, podcasting, and social media management, can generate income from anywhere while building expertise about life in Panama that can be valuable for other expat-focused businesses.

Online training and education platforms that teach practical skills, language learning, or business knowledge can serve international markets while operating from Panama's cost-effective environment. These businesses benefit from the growing demand for online education and the ability to serve students worldwide.

Technology support services for small businesses and fellow expats can provide a steady income while building valuable local business relationships. Many small businesses in Panama need help with technology implementation, website development, or digital marketing, but can't afford large consulting firms.

## Regulatory Considerations and Business Structure

Understanding Panama's regulatory environment is crucial for business success, as compliance requirements vary significantly by business type and can have a substantial impact on profitability and operational flexibility. Getting the regulatory structure right from the beginning prevents expensive corrections later.

Business registration requirements depend on your business type, revenue projections, and operational structure. Some businesses can operate under simplified registration procedures, while others require extensive documentation, professional certifications, or ongoing regulatory compliance. Research these requirements thoroughly before committing to specific business models.

Tax implications vary based on income sources, business structure, and operational details that affect whether your income is considered Panama-source or foreign-source. Professional tax advice is essential because the tax treatment of your business income affects both your Panamanian obligations and your responsibilities in your home country.

Professional licensing requirements apply to many service businesses and can be complex for foreign professionals. Some professions require local certification or validation of foreign credentials, while others may restrict practice to Panamanian citizens or residents with specific visa types.

Employment law becomes relevant if you plan to hire employees, and Panama's labor laws are employee-friendly with significant obligations for employers. Understanding these requirements before hiring prevents legal problems and unexpected costs that can derail business profitability.

Banking and financial compliance requirements affect how you handle business income, international transfers, and tax reporting. Some business models require specific banking arrangements or compliance procedures that aren't obvious until you're operational.

## Building Professional Networks and Partnerships

Business success in Panama often depends on relationships and partnerships more than in many other countries. Building the right professional network can provide access to opportunities, solve operational challenges, and create competitive advantages that aren't available to isolated entrepreneurs.

Local business partnerships can provide market access, regulatory expertise, and operational capabilities that would be expensive or impossible to develop independently. The key is finding partners whose skills and resources complement your own while ensuring that partnership agreements protect your interests and provide clear operational guidelines.

Professional service relationships with attorneys, accountants, and other specialists become crucial as your business grows. These relationships affect everything from regulatory compliance to tax optimization, and the quality of your professional support can determine whether your business thrives or struggles with ongoing operational challenges.

Industry associations and business groups provide networking opportunities, market intelligence, and professional development that can be valuable for business growth. Many sectors have established organizations that can provide access to resources and relationships that would take years to develop independently.

Government relationships, while not required for all businesses, can be valuable for understanding regulatory changes, accessing government contracts, or resolving operational issues that arise during normal business operations. Building these relationships takes time, but they can provide significant advantages when you need them.

International business networks can provide access to markets, suppliers, and partnerships that extend your business reach beyond Panama's borders. Many successful Panama-based businesses serve regional or international markets rather than just local ones.

## Financial Planning for Business Success

Business financial planning in Panama requires understanding both local financial systems and the international implications of generating income while living abroad. Proper financial structure can significantly impact both business success and personal financial security.

Cash flow management becomes crucial because many businesses in Panama experience seasonal fluctuations or irregular payment patterns from clients. Maintaining adequate cash reserves and establishing credit relationships can prevent cash flow problems from derailing otherwise successful operations.

Currency considerations affect businesses that serve international clients but have local operating expenses. While Panama uses the U.S. dollar, international payment processing, banking fees, and tax implications can create currency-related challenges that require careful planning.

Investing business profits requires understanding both Panama's investment opportunities and the tax implications of various investment strategies. Business success should contribute to your overall wealth-building strategy rather than just providing current income.

Retirement planning considerations become important as business income affects both your current lifestyle and your long-term financial security. Business ownership can provide excellent retirement benefits if structured properly, but it requires different planning approaches than traditional employment.

Insurance and risk management for business operations include liability protection, business interruption coverage, and personal insurance that protects your ability to continue operating your business. These considerations become more complex when operating internationally and may require specialized coverage.

## Scaling and Long-Term Growth Strategies

The most successful expat businesses in Panama are built with long-term growth potential, rather than focusing solely on current income generation. Planning for scalability from the beginning creates opportunities for significant wealth building and business value creation.

Systematization and process development allow businesses to grow beyond what the owner can personally handle. This requires documenting procedures, training employees or contractors, and creating systems that can operate consistently without constant personal oversight.

Market expansion strategies might involve serving additional geographic markets, expanding service offerings, or targeting new customer segments. Growth planning should consider both opportunities and the operational capabilities required to serve expanded markets successfully.

Exit strategy planning becomes essential even for businesses you plan to operate long-term because having clear exit options affects business decisions and provides financial security. Some businesses can be sold to others, while some are primarily vehicles for generating income during your residence in Panama.

Succession planning considerations include training replacement management, developing operational systems that can continue without your direct involvement, and creating value that can be transferred to family members or sold to third parties.

Integration with overall wealth strategy ensures that business success contributes to your broader financial goals rather than just providing current income. Successful businesses should build assets, generate cash flow, and create value that supports long-term financial security.

## Looking Forward

Business opportunities in Panama offer genuine potential for building income streams and long-term wealth, but success hinges on understanding local market dynamics, regulatory requirements, and the specific advantages of operating within Panama's unique economic environment. The expats who build successful businesses here are those who identified real problems to solve and structured their operations to take advantage of Panama's strategic advantages.

Your business strategy should align with your overall goals for living in Panama and utilize your specific skills, experience, and market knowledge to achieve them. The goal isn't just to generate income, it's to build something that enhances your life in Panama while providing financial security and growth potential.

The next chapter will delve into advanced logistics and infrastructure optimization, including how to establish systems that support both your lifestyle and business goals while navigating Panama's unique operational environment. Because once you've optimized your finances, built real estate wealth, and established income streams, operational efficiency becomes the key to maintaining and growing everything you've built.

But that's a conversation for next time. For now, consider how your skills, experience, and market knowledge can be applied to address problems in Panama or capitalize on opportunities arising from its strategic location. The best business opportunities often arise from addressing real problems with practical solutions, rather than pursuing abstract business models that sound good in theory but fail to solve actual problems.

# Chapter 4

# Advanced Logistics and Infrastructure Optimization, Building Systems That Work

I was standing in my driveway at 6 AM, waiting for the third different internet technician in two weeks, when I realized that my approach to infrastructure in Panama was fundamentally flawed. I had been treating each service disruption as an isolated problem to be solved rather than understanding that reliable infrastructure in Panama requires building redundant systems and strategic relationships that work together.

The internet had been down for four days, my backup mobile hotspot was throttled to unusable speeds, and I had a critical video conference with U.S. clients in three hours. That morning taught me that a successful expat life in Panama isn't just about finding services that work; it's about creating integrated systems that continue to function even when individual components fail.

After three years of trial and error, I've learned that the expats who thrive in Panama are those who have stopped thinking like consumers and started thinking like infrastructure managers. They don't just buy services, they build systems. They don't just solve problems as they arise; they anticipate potential points of failure and create backup plans before they are needed.

If you're tired of your daily life being disrupted by infrastructure failures and service interruptions, you're ready to learn how to build the operational foundation that supports everything else you want to accomplish in Panama.

# Understanding Panama's Infrastructure Reality

Panama's infrastructure is undergoing rapid development, but it also includes legacy systems that weren't designed to meet current demand levels. This creates a unique environment where some services exceed first-world standards while others operate with third-world reliability. Understanding this mixed reality is crucial for developing systems that operate consistently.

Electricity in Panama comes from a grid that's generally reliable in urban areas but subject to planned outages, voltage fluctuations, and weather-related disruptions that can damage sensitive equipment. The power company often announces planned outages with minimal notice, and unplanned outages can last anywhere from minutes to days, depending on your location and the nature of the problem.

Internet service varies dramatically by provider, location, and service tier, with the added complexity that advertised speeds often bear little resemblance to actual performance during peak usage periods. The infrastructure is in place to provide excellent internet service, but the reality of shared bandwidth and variable maintenance standards means that your connection quality can fluctuate significantly based on factors beyond your control.

Water service reliability depends heavily on your specific location and the age of local infrastructure. Some areas have excellent water pressure and quality, while others experience regular outages, low pressure, or water quality issues that require filtration or treatment. The variability isn't always predictable based on neighborhood quality or property values.

Telecommunications infrastructure includes multiple cellular networks with different coverage areas and reliability patterns. What works well at home might be ineffective at the office, and services that function perfectly under normal conditions may fail during weather events or periods of network congestion. Transportation infrastructure affects everything from daily commuting to receiving deliveries and services. Traffic patterns, road conditions, and public transportation reliability all impact your ability to accomplish routine tasks and can significantly affect the efficiency of services you depend on.

## Building Redundant Communication Systems

Reliable communication becomes critical when you're managing business operations, maintaining relationships with family and clients in other countries, or dealing with the routine emergencies that arise in daily life. Single-point-of-failure communication systems will eventually leave you disconnected at the worst possible moment.

Internet redundancy requires multiple service providers using different infrastructure paths to your location. This means having both cable internet and fiber internet from other companies, or combining fixed wireless with traditional wired service. The key is to ensure that your backup services utilize completely different physical infrastructure, so that construction accidents or infrastructure failures don't eliminate all your options simultaneously.

Mobile connectivity backup should include devices from multiple cellular networks because coverage areas and network reliability vary significantly between providers. Having phones or mobile hotspots from two different carriers provides communication options when one network is experiencing problems or maintenance outages.

Satellite internet backup has become more practical and affordable with services like Starlink, offering connectivity that is independent of local infrastructure. While satellite service may not be suitable for all applications, it can provide essential connectivity during local infrastructure failures or natural disasters.

Voice communication redundancy means having multiple ways to make phone calls that don't all depend on the same infrastructure. This might include landline service, numerous mobile phones, internet-based calling services, and satellite communication options for emergencies.

Emergency communication planning should include methods for contacting family, clients, and service providers even when normal communication channels are disrupted. This includes storing contact information in multiple formats and maintaining backup power sources for communication devices.

## Power Management and Backup Systems

Electrical power in Panama requires active management rather than just plugging things in and expecting them to work reliably. Voltage fluctuations, power outages, and electrical storms all pose threats to expensive equipment and can disrupt business operations or daily life.

Voltage regulation becomes essential for protecting sensitive electronics because Panama's electrical grid experiences voltage fluctuations that can damage computers, appliances, and other expensive equipment. Quality voltage regulators or uninterruptible power supplies can prevent thousands of dollars in equipment damage while ensuring consistent performance.

Backup power systems range from small UPS units that provide battery backup for essential devices to whole-house generators that can maintain normal operations during extended outages. The right solution depends on your specific needs, budget, and the reliability of power service in your area.

Generator selection and installation require understanding your actual power needs, fuel availability, and maintenance requirements. Generators require regular testing and maintenance to function correctly when needed, and fuel storage necessitates proper planning and adherence to safety precautions. Many expats overestimate their power needs, ending up with expensive generators that are costly to operate and maintain.

Battery backup systems for essential devices, such as modems, routers, and phones, can bridge short outages and provide time to start generators during longer ones. Modern lithium battery systems are more reliable and longer-lasting than traditional lead-acid batteries but require a higher initial investment.

Electrical system protection encompasses surge protectors, proper grounding, and electrical panels that can withstand Panama's unique electrical environment. Many homes have electrical systems that weren't designed for modern electronic loads and may need upgrades to operate safely and reliably.

## Water and Waste Management Systems

Water service in Panama requires active management to ensure consistent quality and availability. This includes understanding your local water system, implementing quality control measures, and having backup plans for service interruptions.

Water quality management often requires filtration systems that address specific local water conditions. Some areas have excellent municipal water, while others require extensive treatment to achieve a quality that is acceptable for drinking and cooking. Water testing can identify specific issues that need to be addressed rather than implementing generic filtration systems.

Water storage systems provide backup during service interruptions and can improve water pressure in areas with inconsistent service.

The size and location of storage tanks significantly impact both the practicality and effectiveness of backup water systems. Proper installation is crucial in preventing contamination and minimizing maintenance problems.

Pressure management systems can enhance water pressure throughout your home, ensuring consistent performance for appliances and fixtures that require sufficient pressure. This is particularly important in areas with variable municipal water pressure or homes with complex plumbing systems.

Hot water systems in Panama must account for the high mineral content in some water supplies and the limited need for heating during much of the year. Tank-based systems may be more practical than tankless systems in areas with variable water pressure or quality.

Waste management includes both sewage systems and solid waste disposal, which may not operate according to the standards you're accustomed to. Understanding local systems and having backup plans prevents health hazards and environmental problems.

## Transportation and Logistics Optimization

Efficient transportation affects everything from daily convenience to business operations and emergency preparedness. Building transportation systems that work reliably requires understanding local options and having backup plans for different scenarios.

Vehicle selection and maintenance become more critical in Panama's challenging driving environment. Regular maintenance schedules must account for the unique challenges of tropical climate conditions, the harsher road conditions that can be more detrimental to vehicles, and the availability of parts and service for various vehicle types.

Driver relationships can provide reliable transportation options that don't depend on your personal vehicle availability. Building relationships with trusted drivers provides backup transportation and can be more practical than owning multiple vehicles or depending on ride-sharing services that may not be available when needed.

Delivery and shipping systems require understanding multiple options for receiving packages, mail, and supplies. This includes both international shipping services and local delivery options that can provide goods and services without requiring personal transportation.

Emergency transportation planning should include multiple options for quickly leaving your area in the event of a natural disaster, civil disturbance, or personal emergency. This includes maintaining vehicle fuel reserves, being aware of alternate routes, and having backup transportation arrangements.

Regional transportation understanding aids in planning trips, facilitating business travel, and accessing services that may not be available locally. This includes domestic airline service, bus systems, and ground transportation options for different destinations throughout Panama.

## Financial and Administrative Infrastructure

Managing money, documents, and administrative tasks in Panama requires building systems that work across multiple institutions and account for the complexity of international financial and legal requirements.

Multi-bank relationships provide redundancy for financial services and can improve your access to different services and better terms. Having accounts at multiple banks prevents single-point-of-failure problems and provides options when one institution has issues or policy changes that affect your access.

Document management systems must take into account the importance of physical documents in Panama's legal and administrative systems. This includes secure storage for original documents, backup copies in multiple locations, and systems for organizing and retrieving documents when needed for various transactions.

Professional service relationships with attorneys, accountants, and other specialists need to be maintained even when you don't have immediate needs. These relationships provide access to expertise and services when you need them rather than scrambling to find help during emergencies or time-sensitive situations.

Administrative task scheduling requires an understanding of the operating patterns of government offices, banks, and service providers, allowing you to accomplish routine tasks efficiently. This includes understanding when offices are open, when services are available, and how to minimize time spent on administrative requirements.

International financial coordination involves managing relationships and obligations in both Panama and your home country. This includes understanding reporting requirements, tax obligations, and maintaining access to services in both locations.

## Technology Infrastructure and Digital Systems

Modern expat life relies heavily on technology systems that must function reliably in Panama's environment. This includes both hardware and software solutions that take into account local conditions and international requirements.

Computer and device backup systems ensure that equipment failures don't create major disruptions to work or personal activities. This includes both local backup systems and cloud-based solutions that provide access to data and applications from multiple devices and locations.

Software selection should prioritize applications that work well with variable internet connectivity and can synchronize data across multiple devices and locations. Cloud-based solutions often work better than locally installed software for expats who need access from various locations.

Cybersecurity measures become more critical when operating in international environments with variable network security. This includes VPN services, secure password management, and backup authentication systems that work across different countries and network environments.

Home automation systems can improve efficiency and security, but need to be selected and configured for Panama's electrical and internet environment. Simple, reliable systems often work better than complex installations that require specialized technical support.

Data backup and recovery systems should include both local and international backup options. This protects against both device failures and regional disasters that might affect local infrastructure.

## Health and Safety Infrastructure

Personal safety and health infrastructure requires understanding local resources and building systems that provide security and medical support when needed.

Medical care coordination includes relationships with local healthcare providers, understanding insurance systems, and having backup plans for medical emergencies that require services not available locally. This consists of both routine healthcare and emergency medical evacuation options.

Security systems should be appropriate for your specific location and lifestyle, ranging from basic home security to comprehensive personal security measures. The right approach depends on your location, activities, and risk tolerance rather than generic security recommendations.

Emergency preparedness includes supplies, communication systems, and evacuation plans for different types of emergencies. This requires understanding local risks and having realistic plans for various scenarios, rather than relying on generic emergency preparations.

Personal safety protocols should take into account local conditions and your specific activities and travel patterns. This includes understanding local security situations, having reliable communication methods, and building relationships with local contacts who can assist when needed.

Health monitoring and preventive care become more important when living away from familiar healthcare systems. This includes regular health monitoring, preventive treatments for tropical health risks, and maintaining health records that can be accessed internationally.

## Service Provider Relationship Management

Success in Panama requires building and maintaining relationships with reliable service providers who can handle routine maintenance, emergency repairs, and ongoing services that support your lifestyle and business operations.

Contractor and service provider vetting requires understanding how to evaluate reliability, quality, and pricing in Panama's service environment. This includes checking references, understanding pricing structures, and building trial relationships before committing to major projects or ongoing services.

Maintenance scheduling systems ensure that routine maintenance tasks are completed reliably and help prevent minor problems from becoming major failures. This includes both property maintenance and system maintenance for utilities, vehicles, and equipment.

Emergency service relationships provide access to help during urgent situations that can't wait for normal business hours or routine scheduling. Building these relationships before you need them ensures access to help when problems arise.

Quality control systems help ensure that services meet your standards and that problems are addressed promptly. This includes communication systems for providing feedback and resolving issues before they affect your operations or lifestyle.

Long-term service agreements can provide better service and pricing while ensuring access to providers who understand your specific needs and systems. However, these agreements need to include performance standards and exit provisions that protect your interests.

## Building Integrated Systems

The most successful expat infrastructure systems function as a whole rather than operating as independent components. This integration provides efficiency benefits and prevents single-point-of-failure problems that can disrupt multiple aspects of your life simultaneously.

System redundancy planning ensures that backup systems work when primary systems fail. This requires testing backup systems regularly and ensuring that redundant systems don't share common failure points that could eliminate multiple options simultaneously.

Performance monitoring helps identify problems before they become major failures and provides data for optimizing system performance over time. This includes monitoring both individual system components and overall system performance.

Cost optimization strikes a balance between reliability and cost-effectiveness to build systems that deliver good value while meeting your actual needs. This requires understanding the true costs of system failures and optimizing for the total cost of ownership rather than just the initial cost.

Scalability planning ensures that your infrastructure systems can grow and adapt as your needs change or as Panama's infrastructure develops. Systems that work well for current needs but can't adapt to the evolving requirements may need replacement rather than an upgrade.

Integration with local infrastructure enables improvements to local systems while maintaining backup options for periods when the local infrastructure doesn't meet your needs. This requires staying informed about infrastructure developments and adapting your systems to capitalize on these improvements.

## Looking Forward

Infrastructure optimization in Panama requires a systematic approach to the operational foundation that supports all other objectives. The expats who build successful lives here are those who invest time and money in creating reliable systems, rather than just solving problems as they arise.

Your infrastructure strategy should provide the reliability and functionality necessary to support your lifestyle and business goals, while also accounting for Panama's unique challenges and opportunities. The goal isn't to replicate exactly what you had in your home country; it's to build something that works better for your new situation and environment.

The next chapter will delve into long-term planning and legacy considerations, including estate planning, succession planning, and developing sustainable systems that can support your goals for decades, rather than just the next few years. Once you've optimized your finances, built real estate wealth, established income streams, and created reliable infrastructure systems, long-term planning becomes the key to ensuring that everything you've built continues to work for you and your family over time.

But that's a conversation for next time. For now, start thinking about your current infrastructure systems and identifying single points of failure that could disrupt your life or business operations. The most critical infrastructure investments are often the ones that seem dull until you desperately need them to work.

# Chapter 5

# Long-Term Planning and Legacy Considerations, Building Something That Lasts

I was sitting in my attorney's office in Panama City, reviewing my will, when she asked a question that stopped me cold: "If something happens to you tomorrow, who knows how to access your Panama bank accounts, maintain your property, and handle your business operations?" I had spent three years building a successful expat life with optimized finances, real estate investments, business income, and reliable infrastructure systems. Still, I had never considered what would happen to any of it if I weren't around to manage it personally.

That conversation marked the beginning of understanding that successful expat life in Panama isn't just about building wealth and systems for yourself, it's about creating something sustainable that can survive your absence, benefit your family, and potentially continue generating value long after you're gone. The expats who build truly successful lives here are the ones who think beyond their own needs and create structures that work for multiple generations.

This isn't just about estate planning, though that's certainly part of it. It's about building systems, relationships, and structures that can function independently of your daily management, provide security for your family, and potentially create opportunities for future generations who may or may not choose to continue your Panama adventure.

Suppose you've reached the point where you're thinking beyond just optimizing your current situation and want to build something that lasts. In that case, you're ready to explore the long-term planning strategies that separate temporary expat success from permanent wealth building and legacy creation.

## Understanding Generational Wealth Building

Long-term wealth building in Panama requires shifting from focusing on your financial security to creating assets and systems that can benefit multiple generations. This involves different strategies, different risk profiles, and different legal structures than short-term financial optimization.

Real estate portfolios become foundations for generational wealth when they're structured for long-term ownership rather than short-term returns. This means focusing on properties that will maintain value and generate income for decades, in locations that will remain desirable as Panama develops, and with ownership structures that facilitate transfer to future generations without massive tax implications or legal complications.

Business operations that can function independently of your daily involvement create value that can be transferred, sold, or continued by family members or professional managers. Building businesses with documented systems, trained staff, and operational independence requires different approaches than building businesses that depend on your personal expertise and daily management.

Investment strategies for generational wealth focus on assets that appreciate over decades rather than years, generate reliable income streams, and can be managed by professional advisors when you're no longer able to handle them personally. This includes understanding how different investment vehicles work in Panama's tax environment and how they can be structured for optimal transfer to beneficiaries.

Professional relationships that can outlast your involvement become crucial for maintaining complex financial and business structures over time. This involves establishing relationships with law firms, accounting firms, and other professional service providers that offer institutional stability, rather than relying on individual professionals who may not be available when your family needs their services.

## Estate Planning in Panama's Legal Environment

Estate planning as a foreign resident in Panama involves navigating two or more legal systems simultaneously, and getting this wrong can result in costly delays, unexpected tax obligations, and family conflicts that could have been avoided with proper planning.

Panamanian inheritance law operates according to forced heirship principles, which may differ significantly from the laws in your home country. This means that you cannot freely dispose of all your assets by will; certain portions must be allocated to specific family members, regardless of your preferences. Understanding these requirements and planning around them prevents family conflicts and ensures that your intentions are carried out as much as legally possible.

International estate planning requires coordinating your Panama estate plan with estate planning in your home country and any other countries where you have assets or tax obligations. This coordination affects not just the distribution of assets but also the tax treatment of inheritances and the procedures that beneficiaries must follow to claim their inheritances.

Trust structures can provide significant advantages for estate planning in Panama. Still, they require careful structuring to achieve your goals while complying with both Panamanian law and the laws of your home country. Trusts can provide asset protection, tax advantages, and operational continuity that aren't available through simple wills, but they also require ongoing administration and compliance that adds complexity and cost.

Corporate ownership structures for real estate and business assets can facilitate estate planning by allowing ownership interests to be transferred more easily than direct ownership of assets. However, corporate structures also create ongoing compliance obligations and may have tax implications that need to be considered in the overall estate planning strategy.

Power of attorney documents become crucial for managing your affairs if you become incapacitated, and Panama's legal system has specific requirements for these documents that may be different from your home country. Having properly prepared and executed power of attorney documents prevents family members from having to go through costly and time-consuming legal procedures to manage your affairs during emergencies.

## Business Succession and Continuity Planning

If you've built successful business operations in Panama, planning for their continuation or transition is essential to protect the value you've created and provide ongoing benefits for your family. This requires different strategies depending on whether you want the business to continue operating, be sold, or be liquidated.

Management succession planning involves identifying and training people who can run your business operations if you're unable to continue doing so personally. This might include family members, key employees, or professional managers, but it requires documenting systems and procedures that allow the business to continue operating without your daily involvement.

Ownership transition strategies determine how business ownership will be transferred and what happens to business operations during the transition period. This includes valuation procedures for determining fair compensation for business interests, financing arrangements for ownership transfers, and legal structures that facilitate smooth transitions while protecting family interests.

Key relationship preservation ensures that your business's valuable relationships with clients, suppliers, vendors, and service providers can be maintained through ownership or management transitions. This requires documenting relationships, introducing successors to key contacts, and ensuring that transition procedures don't disrupt business operations.

Financial structure optimization may involve restructuring business finances to facilitate succession planning while optimizing tax treatment for both current operations and future transfers. This may include modifying corporate structures, adjusting debt arrangements, or revising operational procedures to enhance transferability.

Exit strategy implementation provides alternatives to succession planning by creating procedures for selling business operations or liquidating business assets in a manner that maximizes value for beneficiaries. This includes identifying potential buyers, preparing businesses for sale, and structuring transactions to optimize tax treatment and minimize transition costs.

## Family Wealth Management and Education

Successful long-term planning requires preparing family members to manage and benefit from the wealth and systems you've created. This involves both financial education and practical training in managing assets and relationships in Panama's unique environment.

Financial literacy education for family members should include understanding Panama's financial systems, tax implications of different types of assets and income, and the operational requirements for maintaining real estate, business operations, and investment portfolios. This education needs to be ongoing and practical rather than theoretical.

Cultural and language preparation helps family members who may need to manage Panama-based assets understand local customs, language requirements, and relationship management approaches that are essential for maintaining business and professional relationships over time. This includes understanding how business is conducted in Panama and the importance of personal relationships in accomplishing objectives.

Professional relationship introductions ensure that family members have access to the attorneys, accountants, property managers, and other service providers who will be essential for managing inherited assets. These introductions should happen while you're still actively involved so that relationships can develop naturally rather than being forced during crisis situations.

Decision-making frameworks provide family members with structured approaches for making complex decisions about asset management, business operations, and long-term planning. This includes establishing family governance structures, communication procedures, and conflict resolution mechanisms that can prevent family disputes from damaging valuable assets.

Gradual responsibility transfer allows family members to develop skills and confidence in managing Panama-based assets while you're still available to provide guidance and support. This practical training is often more valuable than theoretical education and helps identify potential problems before they become serious issues.

# International Tax and Compliance Planning

Long-term planning for expats involves managing tax and compliance obligations that may extend far beyond your lifetime and affect beneficiaries who may live in different countries and have different tax situations than your own.

Multi-generational tax planning requires understanding how different assets and income streams will be taxed in the hands of beneficiaries who may be subject to different tax rules than you are. This includes understanding inheritance tax implications, income tax treatment of inherited assets, and reporting requirements that beneficiaries will need to comply with. Treaty benefits and international agreements may provide opportunities for tax optimization that aren't available under domestic tax rules alone. However, these benefits often have specific requirements and limitations that need to be understood and planned for in advance rather than addressed reactively.

Compliance system documentation ensures that family members understand reporting requirements, filing deadlines, and record-keeping obligations that will be necessary for maintaining compliance with tax and regulatory requirements in multiple countries. This documentation should include procedures, contact information, and schedules that allow smooth continuation of compliance activities.

Professional service coordination between advisors in different countries becomes essential for managing complex international tax situations that involve multiple jurisdictions. This requires establishing relationships and communication procedures that allow advisors to work together effectively rather than creating conflicting advice or duplicated efforts.

Regular review and updating procedures ensure that tax and compliance strategies remain current as laws change, family situations evolve, and asset structures develop over time. This includes establishing schedules for review meetings, updating documentation, and modifying strategies based on changing circumstances.

## Community Integration and Social Legacy

Building a lasting presence in Panama involves more than just financial and legal structures; it includes developing community relationships and social connections that provide mutual benefits and create positive impacts that extend beyond your interests.

Community involvement through volunteer work, charitable giving, or civic participation creates relationships and a reputation that can benefit both you and your family over time. These relationships often provide practical benefits through access to information, services, and opportunities that aren't available through purely commercial relationships.

Charitable structure development allows you to formalize your community involvement while potentially achieving tax benefits and creating a lasting impact through organized giving. Panama's legal system provides options for charitable giving that can be incorporated into overall estate planning while supporting causes that are important to you.

Cultural bridge building between expat and local communities creates value for everyone involved and can provide your family with deeper integration into Panamanian society. This might involve language exchange programs, cultural events, or business relationships that provide mutual benefits while building lasting connections.

Educational and mentorship opportunities allow you to share knowledge and experiencc with other expats while building relationships that can provide ongoing benefits for your family.

This includes formal mentorship through organizations as well as informal relationship building through shared activities and common interests.

Legacy project development might involve creating lasting contributions to your community through infrastructure improvements, educational programs, or cultural initiatives that provide ongoing benefits while establishing your family's positive reputation in the community.

## Risk Management and Contingency Planning

Long-term planning requires preparing for scenarios that may be unlikely but could have serious consequences for your family and the assets you've built. Comprehensive risk management addresses both predictable challenges and unexpected disasters that could disrupt your plans.

Political and economic risk assessment involves understanding potential changes in Panama's political or economic environment that could affect your assets or your family's ability to maintain them. This includes diversification strategies that provide protection against local risks while maintaining the benefits of Panama-based assets.

Natural disaster preparedness includes both immediate emergency planning and long-term recovery strategies that ensure your assets and family can recover from hurricanes, earthquakes, floods, or other natural disasters that could affect Panama. This includes insurance coverage, backup documentation, and recovery procedures.

Health and disability planning addresses scenarios where you might become unable to manage your affairs due to illness, injury, or cognitive decline. This includes healthcare directives, disability insurance, and management succession procedures that can be implemented quickly when needed.

Family dispute resolution mechanisms provide structured approaches for resolving conflicts that might arise among family members regarding asset management, business operations, or inheritance distributions. Having these mechanisms in place before conflicts arise can prevent disputes from damaging valuable assets or family relationships.

Emergency liquidity planning ensures that your family has access to cash and liquid assets during emergencies when other assets might not be readily accessible. This includes maintaining emergency funds, establishing credit facilities, and creating procedures for quick asset liquidation when necessary.

## Technology and Documentation Systems

Long-term planning requires creating documentation and systems that can be understood and maintained by people other than yourself. This includes both digital systems and physical documentation that provide access to information and resources when needed.

Digital asset management involves organizing and documenting online accounts, digital files, and electronic systems that are essential for managing your assets and operations. This includes password management, account documentation, and procedures for accessing digital resources during emergencies.

Physical document organization and storage ensure that important papers, contracts, and legal documents are properly preserved and accessible when needed. This includes both original documents and backup copies stored in multiple secure locations with clear instructions for access.

Information system documentation provides instructions and procedures for using the various systems and relationships that support your operations. This includes contact information, procedural instructions, and troubleshooting guidance that allows others to maintain your systems when you're not available.

Regular backup and update procedures ensure that documentation remains current and accessible as systems change and develop over time. This includes both digital backups and physical document management with scheduled reviews and updates.

Access control and security measures protect sensitive information while ensuring that authorized family members and advisors can access what they need when they need it. This balance between security and accessibility requires careful planning and regular review.

## Monitoring and Adjustment Strategies

Long-term planning is not a one-time activity but an ongoing process that requires regular review and adjustment as circumstances change, laws evolve, and family situations develop. Building systems for ongoing management ensures that your plans remain effective over time.

Regular review schedules ensure that estate plans, business structures, and financial strategies are updated as needed to remain effective and compliant with current laws and regulations. This includes annual reviews with professional advisors and more frequent monitoring of key indicators and performance metrics.

Performance measurement systems help track whether your long-term planning strategies are achieving their intended goals and identify areas where adjustments might be needed. This includes both financial performance measures and operational effectiveness indicators.

Family communication procedures ensure that family members stay informed about plans, changes, and their own responsibilities within the overall strategy. Regular family meetings and communication help prevent misunderstandings and ensure that everyone understands their roles and responsibilities.

Professional advisor coordination ensures that your various advisors work together effectively and that changes made by one advisor don't create problems for other aspects of your planning. This requires establishing communication procedures and coordination mechanisms among your advisory team.

Flexibility and adaptation planning build in the ability to modify strategies and structures as circumstances change rather than being locked into approaches that may become obsolete or counterproductive over time. This includes building flexibility into legal structures and maintaining options for future changes.

## Looking Forward

Long-term planning and legacy creation in Panama represent the culmination of successful expat life, the transition from building personal financial security to creating something that can benefit multiple generations and contribute positively to your adopted community. This requires different thinking, different strategies, and different professional relationships than short-term optimization, but it provides the foundation for truly lasting success.

Your long-term planning should integrate all the elements of successful expat life, optimized finances, real estate wealth, business income, reliable infrastructure, and sustainable systems into a cohesive strategy that can function independently of your daily management while providing ongoing benefits for your family and community.

The strategies and structures you implement for long-term planning will determine whether the success you've built in

Panama continues to grow and benefit others long after you're gone, or whether it becomes a burden that family members struggle to maintain or eventually abandon. The difference lies in thinking beyond your own needs and building something truly sustainable.

This concludes our series on advanced living abroad. We've covered the progression from basic expat survival to sophisticated wealth building and legacy planning, focusing on strategies that take advantage of Panama's unique opportunities while managing its specific challenges. The expats who build truly successful lives here are the ones who approach each stage systematically and build on previous achievements to create something greater than the sum of its parts.

Your Panama journey doesn't end with implementing these strategies; it evolves into maintaining and improving them while helping others who are following similar paths. The knowledge and experience you've gained become valuable assets that can benefit both your own family and the broader expat community that helped you succeed.

# Conclusion

# From Survival to Legacy, What Advanced Expat Living Means

I was having coffee with a friend who had just completed his first year in Panama, listening to him complain about internet outages, banking frustrations, and the general chaos of expat life, when I realized how far I'd traveled since my early days here. Not geographically, we were sitting in the same café where I used to vent my frustrations six years ago, but in terms of understanding what it means to live successfully as an expat in Panama.

His problems were real, and I remembered them well: the internet cutting out during important calls, banks that seemed designed to make simple transactions complicated, and the constant feeling that you're one bureaucratic mistake away from disaster. But what struck me was how different my perspective had become. Where he saw problems to be endured, I now saw systems to be optimized. Where he felt frustrated by complexity, I had learned to see opportunity.

That conversation reminded me why I started this series. There's a crucial difference between surviving as an expat and thriving as one, and that difference isn't just about time or luck. It's about understanding that advanced expat living isn't simply an extension of beginner expat living; it's an entirely different approach to building a life abroad.

After walking through financial optimization, real estate strategies, business development, infrastructure systems, and legacy planning together, it's time to step back and examine what we've been discussing: the transformation from tourist thinking to resident thinking to investor thinking to legacy thinking. Each stage requires different skills, different relationships, and fundamentally different ways of approaching problems and opportunities.

## The Four Stages of Expat Evolution

Most expats never progress beyond the first stage, and many who do make it further stop before reaching their full potential. Understanding these stages helps you recognize where you are and what you need to focus on next.

**Stage One: Survival Mode.** This is where everyone starts, and where many people stay. You're focused on basic needs: finding a place to live, figuring out how to buy groceries, navigating simple transactions, and dealing with immediate problems as they arise. Your mindset is reactive; issues occur, and you solve them. Success is measured by your ability to handle daily life without major disasters.

The danger of staying in survival mode is that you never build anything sustainable. You're always one problem away from crisis, always dependent on others for help, and always paying premium prices because you don't understand how systems work. Survival mode thinking treats Panama like a complicated version of home rather than understanding it as a completely different environment with its own logic and opportunities.

**Stage Two: Optimization Mode.** This is where our series began, the transition from surviving to optimizing. You've figured out the basics, and now you're focused on making your money work better, finding more efficient ways to handle routine tasks, and building systems that reduce friction in your daily life. Your mindset becomes proactive; you anticipate problems and create solutions before you need them.

Financial optimization, smart banking relationships, efficient service provider networks, and systematic approaches to routine tasks all characterize this stage. You stop paying the "gringo tax" because you understand local systems well enough to navigate them efficiently. Success is measured by your ability to live better for less money while reducing the time and energy spent on administrative tasks.

**Stage Three: Growth Mode.** This is where expat life becomes genuinely exciting. You're not just optimizing what you brought from home; you're building new sources of value that didn't exist before you moved to Panama. Real estate investments, business development, strategic partnerships, and wealth-building activities that capitalize on Panama's unique opportunities become your focus.

Your mindset shifts from protecting what you have to growing what you can build. You start thinking like an investor rather than a consumer, looking for ways to create value rather than just preserving it. Success is measured by your ability to build assets and income streams that wouldn't have been possible in your home country.

**Stage Four: Legacy Mode.** This is the stage most expats never reach, but it represents the ultimate expression of successful expat living. You're not just building wealth for yourself; you're creating systems, relationships, and structures that can benefit others and continue beyond your involvement. Generational wealth building, community contribution, mentorship of other expats, and creating a lasting positive impact become priorities.

Your mindset becomes generational, you're building something that will outlast you and contribute to both your family's future and the broader community you've joined. Success is measured by the sustainability and positive impact of what you've created, not just its current value to you personally.

# What We've Been Building

Looking back through our five chapters, I realize we weren't just discussing tactics for expat living; we were building a comprehensive system for transforming yourself from a foreigner trying to recreate home to a resident who has become an integral part of Panama's economic and social ecosystem.

**Financial Optimization** provided us with a solid foundation, enabling us to understand how to optimize our finances within Panama's unique tax and banking environment while fulfilling our obligations elsewhere. But more than that, it taught us to think strategically about money in ways that take advantage of opportunities that don't exist in our home countries.

**Real Estate Strategies** showed us how to build wealth through Panama's property markets, but it also demonstrated the importance of understanding local market dynamics rather than imposing assumptions from elsewhere. The real lesson was learning to see opportunities that are invisible to people who think like tourists.

**Business Development** introduced income generation strategies, but the deeper insight was about identifying problems that need solving and positioning ourselves to solve them. The most successful expat businesses aren't transplanted versions of home country businesses; they're solutions to specifically Panamanian problems or ways to leverage Panama's strategic advantages.

**Infrastructure Optimization** addressed the practical systems that support everything else, but it taught us to think like infrastructure managers rather than consumers. Instead of just buying services, we learned to build redundant systems that continue functioning even when individual components fail.

**Legacy Planning** covered estate planning and wealth transfer, but the real focus was on building something sustainable that provides value beyond our lifetime. This is where expat living transitions from personal optimization to community contribution.

## The Integration Challenge

The biggest mistake I see advanced expats make is treating these different areas as separate projects rather than integrated components of a comprehensive life strategy. Your financial optimization should support your real estate strategy, which should align with your business development, which should be built on reliable infrastructure, which should all be structured for long-term sustainability.

This integration is what separates successful expats from those who build impressive individual achievements but never create coherent, sustainable success. The expats who thrive long-term are those who understand that everything connects to everything else, and that optimization in one area creates opportunities in others.

For example, your banking relationships affect your real estate financing options, which influence your property investment strategy, which impacts your rental income, which provides capital for business development, which generates cash flow that supports infrastructure improvements, which enhances the value of everything you've built. Understanding these connections allows you to make decisions that create multiplicative rather than additive value.

## The Relationship Revolution

Perhaps the most critical insight from our journey is understanding that advanced expat success depends more on relationships than on systems, more on trust than on contracts, and more on integration into local networks than on importing solutions from home.

Every successful strategy we've discussed, from tax optimization to real estate investment to business development, ultimately depends on relationships with local professionals who understand both the opportunities and the obstacles that aren't obvious to outsiders. The expats who build lasting success are those who invest time and energy in building these relationships before they need them, rather than scrambling to find help during crises.

But relationships in Panama work differently than they might in your home country. They're more personal, more long-term oriented, and based more on mutual benefit and trust than on formal contracts and legal structures. Understanding this difference and adapting your approach accordingly can mean the difference between success and frustration.

The most successful expats I know have stopped thinking of themselves as foreigners living in Panama and started thinking of themselves as Panamanians who happen to have foreign backgrounds. This mental shift affects everything from how you approach business relationships to how you structure long-term planning.

## Common Advanced Expat Mistakes

After watching hundreds of expats progress through these stages, I've noticed patterns in the mistakes that derail advanced expat success. Understanding these mistakes can help you avoid them or recognize them early enough to make corrections.

**Mistake #1: Optimizing for the Wrong Metrics.** Many expats focus on minimizing costs rather than maximizing value, or on short-term gains rather than long-term wealth building. The goal isn't to live as cheaply as possible; it's to live as well as possible while building something sustainable. Sometimes this means spending more money upfront to create systems that generate better long-term results.

**Mistake #2: Trying to Recreate Home.** Advanced expats sometimes make the mistake of using sophisticated tools to recreate familiar systems rather than building new systems that work better in Panama's environment. The most successful strategies often look nothing like what worked in your home country because they're designed specifically for Panama's opportunities and challenges.

**Mistake #3: Underestimating Complexity.** Panama offers genuine opportunities for advanced strategies, but these opportunities come with complexity that can be expensive if you don't understand them properly. The expats who get into trouble are often those who pursue sophisticated strategies without investing in the professional support needed to implement them correctly.

**Mistake #4: Neglecting Integration.** Building separate systems for finances, real estate, business, and infrastructure without ensuring they work together efficiently creates inefficiencies and missed opportunities. The most successful expats think holistically about how different components of their Panama life support and enhance each other.

**Mistake #5: Forgetting the Human Element.** All the systems and strategies in the world don't matter if you haven't built the relationships needed to maintain them over time. Panama is a relationship-driven culture, and sustainable success requires understanding and adapting to this reality rather than trying to operate purely through formal systems.

## What Advanced Expat Living Looks Like

After three years of implementing these strategies and working with other expats at various stages of this journey, I can tell you that advanced expat living doesn't look like what most people expect when they first move to Panama.

It doesn't look like sitting on a beach sipping cocktails while your investments automatically generate passive income. It doesn't look like avoiding all the complexities of Panama's systems by hiring others to handle everything for you. And it doesn't look like recreating your home country lifestyle in a tropical setting.

Instead, advanced expat living looks like having systems that work reliably, relationships that provide value and support, multiple sources of income that aren't all dependent on your home country's economy, and the flexibility to take advantage of opportunities as they arise. It looks like being able to travel for weeks or months without worrying about whether your business operations, property management, or financial systems will continue functioning smoothly.

Most importantly, it looks like being able to contribute value to your adopted community rather than just consuming resources from it. The most successful advanced expats I know are those who have become assets to Panama rather than just residents of Panama.

## The Mindset Shift That Changes Everything

The fundamental difference between basic expat living and advanced expat living isn't about specific strategies or tactics; it's about a fundamental shift in how you think about your relationship with Panama and your role in the community you've joined.

Basic expat thinking focuses on what Panama can do for you: lower cost of living, better weather, simpler lifestyle, tax advantages, or whatever benefits attracted you initially. This consumer mindset treats Panama as a service provider and you as a customer who pays for benefits received.

Advanced expat thinking focuses on what you can contribute to Panama: skills, knowledge, capital, connections, or other resources that create value for others while building your wealth and security. This investor/contributor mindset treats Panama as a partner and yourself as someone who creates mutual benefit through your activities and investments.

This shift affects everything from how you approach business opportunities to how you structure your finances to how you build relationships with local professionals. It's the difference between trying to extract maximum value from Panama and trying to create maximum value within Panama.

## Building Your Advanced Expat Strategy

If you're ready to progress beyond basic expat survival and start building something more substantial, the first step is honestly assessing which stage you're currently in and what you need to focus on next.

Most second-year expats are ready to begin financial optimization but may not yet have the foundation of relationships and systems understanding needed for more advanced strategies. There's no shame in taking time to build a solid foundation before moving to more complex approaches.

The key is to approach each stage systematically rather than trying to jump ahead to strategies that require foundation work you haven't completed yet. A solid understanding of Panama's banking system is essential before attempting sophisticated tax optimization. Reliable infrastructure systems are necessary before launching complex business operations. Proven real estate investment experience should precede major portfolio expansion.

But within each stage, the most critical work is often the least visible: building relationships, understanding local dynamics, and developing the reputation and trust that make advanced strategies possible. This relationship work takes time and can't be rushed, but it's the foundation that determines whether your advanced strategy will succeed or fail.

## The Long View

Perhaps the most critical insight from our journey is understanding that successful expat living is a long-term game. The strategies that work best often take years to develop fully, and the most valuable opportunities are usually available only to people who have proven their commitment to staying and contributing.

This long-term perspective affects how you approach everything from banking relationships to property investments to business development. Short-term thinking leads to decisions that optimize for immediate benefits but limit long-term opportunities. Long-term thinking accepts short-term costs and complexity in exchange for building something truly valuable over time.

The expats who build the most successful lives in Panama are those who committed early to making Panama their permanent home rather than just a temporary destination. This commitment affects how others perceive you, what opportunities become available, and how seriously local professionals take your requests for advice and service.

## What Comes Next

Completing Panama 201 doesn't mean you've learned everything there is to know about advanced expat living; it means you've developed the framework and foundation for continuing to learn and grow. The specific tactics and strategies we've discussed will evolve as Panama's economy develops, regulations change, and your personal situation changes.

What won't change is the fundamental approach: systematic thinking, relationship building, integration with local systems, and long-term perspective. These principles will serve you well regardless of how specific circumstances evolve.

The most successful advanced expats I know are those who continue learning, adapting their strategies as circumstances change, and sharing their knowledge with others who are following similar paths. This community of experienced expats serves as both a resource for ongoing learning and a means to contribute to others' success.

## Your Panama Legacy

As we conclude this series, I want to leave you with a challenge that goes beyond personal optimization: What legacy will you create through your Panama experience?

The most fulfilling advanced expat lives are built by people who used their success in Panama as a platform for creating value that extends beyond their interests. This might involve mentoring other expats, contributing to local economic development, supporting charitable causes, or building businesses that provide employment and opportunities for local residents.

Your Panama legacy isn't just about what you build for yourself and your family; it's about how your presence in Panama makes the country better for others, both expats and locals, who come after you. This perspective transforms advanced expat living from a personal optimization project into a community contribution project.

The strategies we've discussed throughout Panama 201 provide the tools and framework for building wealth, security, and comfort as an expat in Panama. But how you use those tools to create value for others will determine whether your expat experience represents just personal success or something more meaningful.

Six years ago, I came to Panama looking for a better life for myself. What I found was the opportunity to build something that provides value for others while creating security and satisfaction for my own family. That discovery transformed not just my financial situation but my entire understanding of what it means to live successfully abroad.

The same opportunities are available to you, but only if you're willing to think beyond personal optimization and start building something that contributes to the community you've joined. That's the real meaning of advanced expat living: using your success as a platform for creating value that extends far beyond your interests.

Panama has allowed all of us to build something better than what we left behind. What we do with that opportunity will determine not just our success, but the success of the expat community and the broader Panamanian community we've chosen to join.

The journey from survival to legacy is long and challenging, but it's also the most rewarding adventure you'll ever undertake. Welcome to the advanced expat community. The real work starts now.

# Acknowledgments

This guide exists because of the generosity of countless people who shared their experiences, mistakes, and hard-won wisdom about life in Panama.

## To the Panama Expat Community

First, to the thousands of expats in Facebook groups, forums, and coffee shops across Panama who answered endless questions, shared their stories, and proved that the expat community is as welcoming as advertised. Your willingness to help strangers navigate everything from visa paperwork to finding the best mechanic in David made this guide possible.

Special thanks to the veteran expats who've been here long enough to see the patterns, who could distinguish between the challenges that matter and the ones that don't, and who shared the kind of honest perspective that only comes from years of actual living here, not just visiting.

## To the Professionals

To the immigration lawyers, real estate agents, accountants, and other professionals who patiently explained complex processes and corrected my misconceptions. Your expertise turned what could have been generic advice into actionable guidance.

To the healthcare professionals who helped demystify Panama's medical system, and to the business owners who shared the real numbers behind cost-of-living estimates, numbers that reflect what expats spend, not what tourism websites claim.

## To Early Readers and Contributors

To those who read early drafts and told me when something didn't make sense, when I was being too optimistic, or when I'd missed something important. Your feedback transformed scattered observations into a coherent guide.

To the expats who shared their first-year stories, both the successes and the frustrations, with remarkable honesty. Your experiences became the reality checks that make this guide different from the usual "paradise found" narratives.

## To Family and Friends

To my family, especially Paula and the E-tribe, who supported this project even when it meant countless hours of "just five more minutes" while I finished another section. Your patience, understanding, and support with my Panama obsession made this possible and have not gone unnoticed.

To friends who listened to more Panama stories than anyone should have to endure, and who asked the practical questions that helped shape what information needed to be included.

## To Future Panama Expats

Finally, to everyone who will read this guide and make their own Panama journey. Your questions and experiences will undoubtedly reveal gaps in this information and new insights worth sharing. The Panama expat community grows stronger when we all contribute what we learn.

This guide reflects the collective wisdom of hundreds of people who chose to share their knowledge rather than keep it to themselves. That generosity of spirit is one of the best things about the Panama expat experience.

## A Note on Omissions

If I've failed to mention someone who contributed to this guide, it's an oversight of memory, not a lack of gratitude. The Panama expat community is large and generous, and every conversation, every shared experience, and every piece of advice helped shape this resource.

---

*The information in this guide is current as of 2025, but Panama, like any country, continues to evolve. Future editions will benefit from the experiences of readers who take this advice and make it work in their own lives.*

# Connect With Elwood Fletcher

Stay connected and follow Elwood's journey as he explores Panama and shares tips, stories, and more.

## Website & Store

www.Elwoods-Expat-Essentials.com

## Blog

panamabeginnersguide.wordpress.com

## Social Media

Follow Elwood on all his platforms for daily updates, fun insights, and exclusive content.

**Facebook**: @ElwoodEats
**Instagram**: @ElwoodEats
**BlueSky**: @ElwoodEats
**Mastodon**: @ElwoodEats
**Tumblr**: @ElwoodEats
**Threads**: @ElwoodEats
**LinkedIn**: @ElwoodFletcher
**X**: @ElwoodEats

## Patreon

Support Elwood's work and get exclusive content, tips, and much more!

patreon.com/ElwoodFletcher

# Contact

For inquiries, collaborations, or to say hello, feel free to reach out.

Elwood@Elwoods-Expat-Essentials.com

# Elwood Fletcher

Explorer | Foodie | Panama Enthusiast | Expat Life Advocate

www.ingramcontent.com/pod-product-compliance
Lightning Source LLC
LaVergne TN
LVHW090329210926
848480LV00004B/1348

* 9 7 9 8 2 3 1 2 6 8 6 1 0 *